GRAPHIC LIBRARY™

GRAPHIC HISTORY

The SALEM WITCH TRIALS

by Michael Martin

illustrated by Brian Bascle

Consultant:
Walter W. Woodward
Assistant Professor of History
University of Connecticut, Hartford

Raintree

www.raintreepublishers.co.uk
Visit our website to find out
more information about
Raintree books.

To order:
☎ Phone 0845 6044371
🖶 Fax +44 (0) 1865 312263
✉ Email myorders@raintreepublishers.co.uk

Customers from outside the UK please telephone +44 1865 312262

Raintree is an imprint of Capstone Global Library Limited, a company incorporated in England and Wales having its registered office at 7 Pilgrim Street, London, EC4V 6LB – Registered company number: 6695582

Text © Capstone Press 2005
First published in hardback in the United Kingdom by Capstone Global Library in 2011
The moral rights of the proprietor have been asserted.

Art Directors: Jason Knudson and Heather Kindseth
Editorial Director: Blake A. Hoena
Storyboard Artist: Jason Knudson
Illustrator: Brian Bascle
Editors: Rebecca Glaser and John-Paul Wilkins
Originated by Capstone Global Library
Printed and bound in China by South China Printing Company Ltd

Acknowledgements
We would like to thank Philip Charles Crawford for his assistance in the preparation of this book.

ISBN 978 1 406 22558 7 (hardback)
15 14 13 12 11
10 9 8 7 6 5 4 3 2 1

British Library Cataloguing in Publication Data
Martin, Michael.
The Salem Witch Trials. -- (Graphic history)
133.4'3'097445-dc22
A full catalogue record for this book is available from the British Library.

Disclaimer
All the internet addresses (URLs) given in this book were valid at the time of going to press. However, due to the dynamic nature of the internet, some addresses may have changed, or sites may have changed or ceased to exist since publication. While the author and publisher regret any inconvenience this may cause readers, no responsibility for any such changes can be accepted by either the author or the publisher.

Editor's note: Direct quotations from primary sources are indicated by a yellow background.

Direct quotations appear on the following pages:
Pages 5, 23, from Samuel Parris' sermons, quoted in *A Delusion of Satan*, Frances Hill (Doubleday, 1995).
Pages 6, 21, from Cotton Mather's *Memorable Providences, Relating to Witchcrafts and Possessions*.
Pages 8, 11, 12, 24, from *The Salem Witchcraft Papers*, edited by Paul Boyer and Stephen Nissenbaum
    (University of Virginia Library. http://etext.virginia.edu/salem/witchcraft/texts/transcripts.html)
Page 25, from Increase Mather's "Cases of Conscience Concerning Evil Spirits Personating Men," quoted in
    Delusion of Satan, Frances Hill (Doubleday, 1995).
Page 27, from Ann Putnam's apology in 1706, quoted in *A Delusion of Satan*, Frances Hill (Doubleday, 1995).

Contents

CHAPTER · 1

Strange Behaviour in Salem

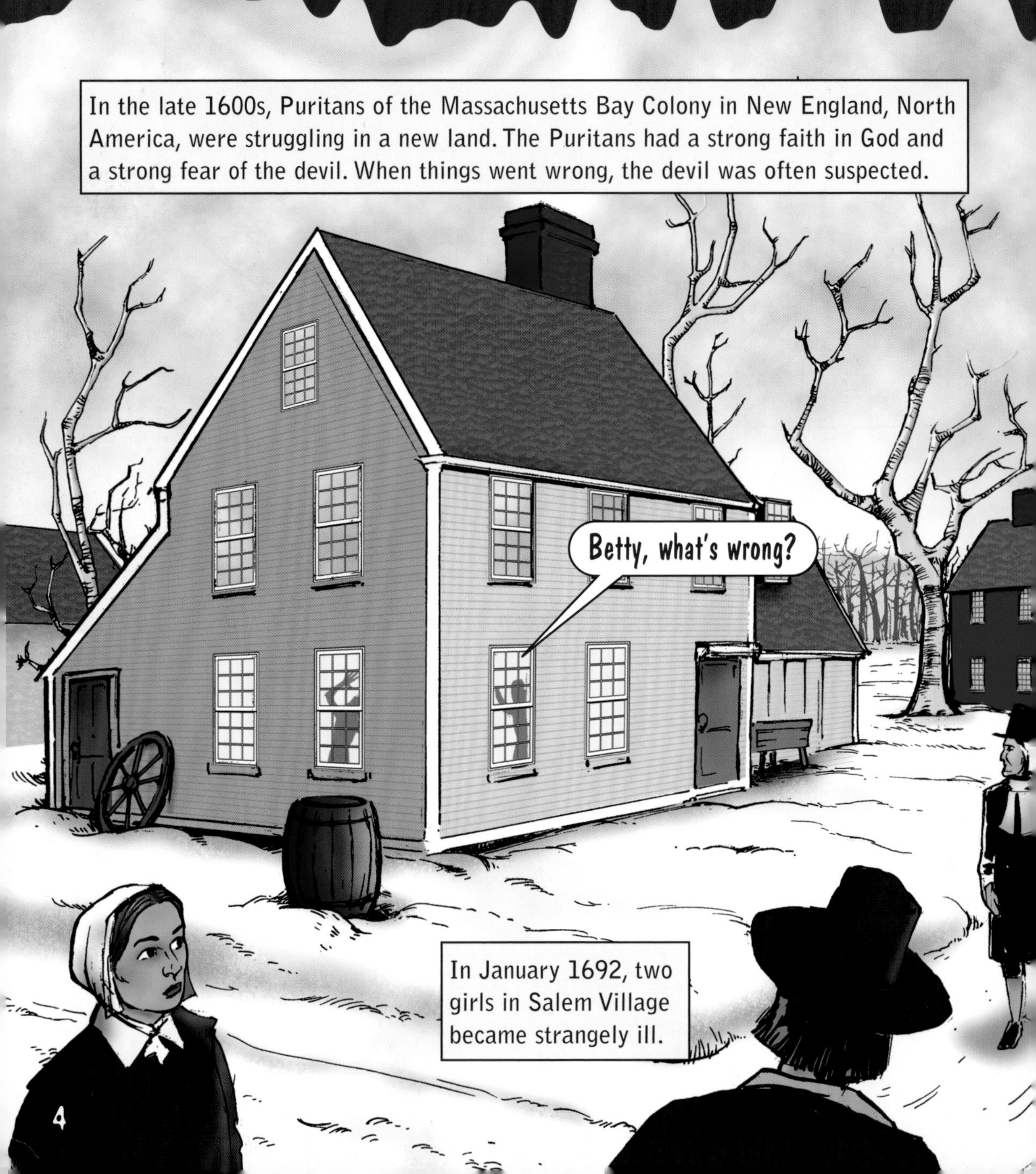
In the late 1600s, Puritans of the Massachusetts Bay Colony in New England, North America, were struggling in a new land. The Puritans had a strong faith in God and a strong fear of the devil. When things went wrong, the devil was often suspected.
Betty, what's wrong?
In January 1692, two girls in Salem Village became strangely ill.

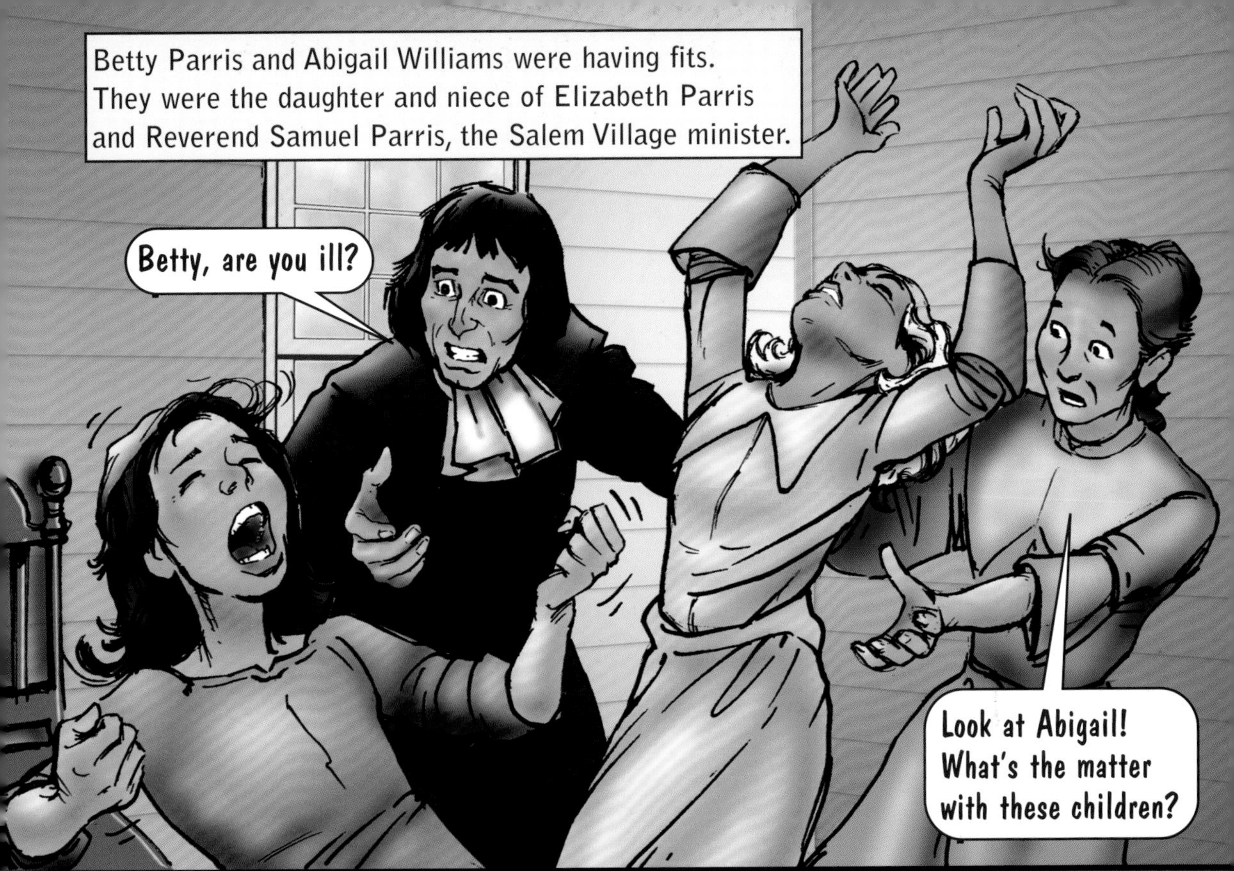
Betty Parris and Abigail Williams were having fits. They were the daughter and niece of Elizabeth Parris and Reverend Samuel Parris, the Salem Village minister.
Betty, are you ill?
Look at Abigail! What's the matter with these children?

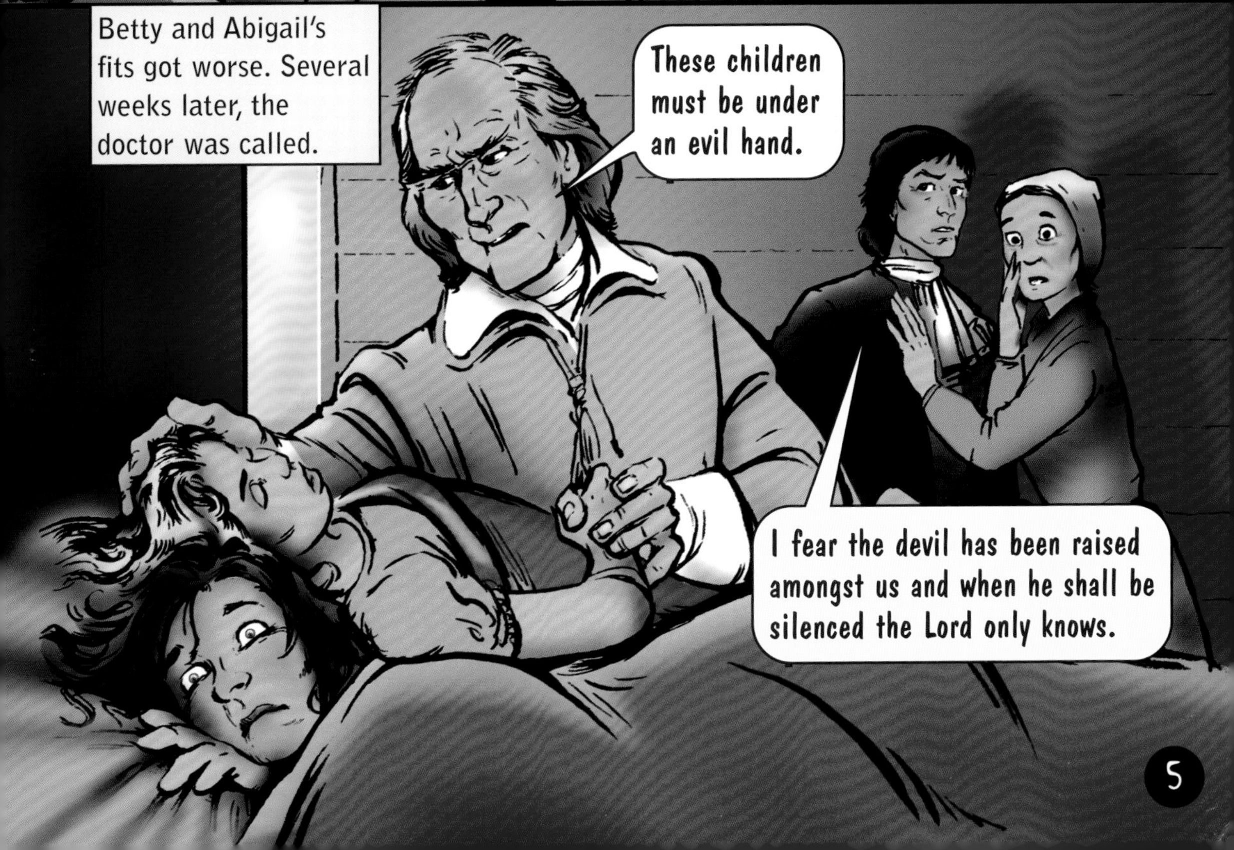
Betty and Abigail's fits got worse. Several weeks later, the doctor was called.
These children must be under an evil hand.
I fear the devil has been raised amongst us and when he shall be silenced the Lord only knows.

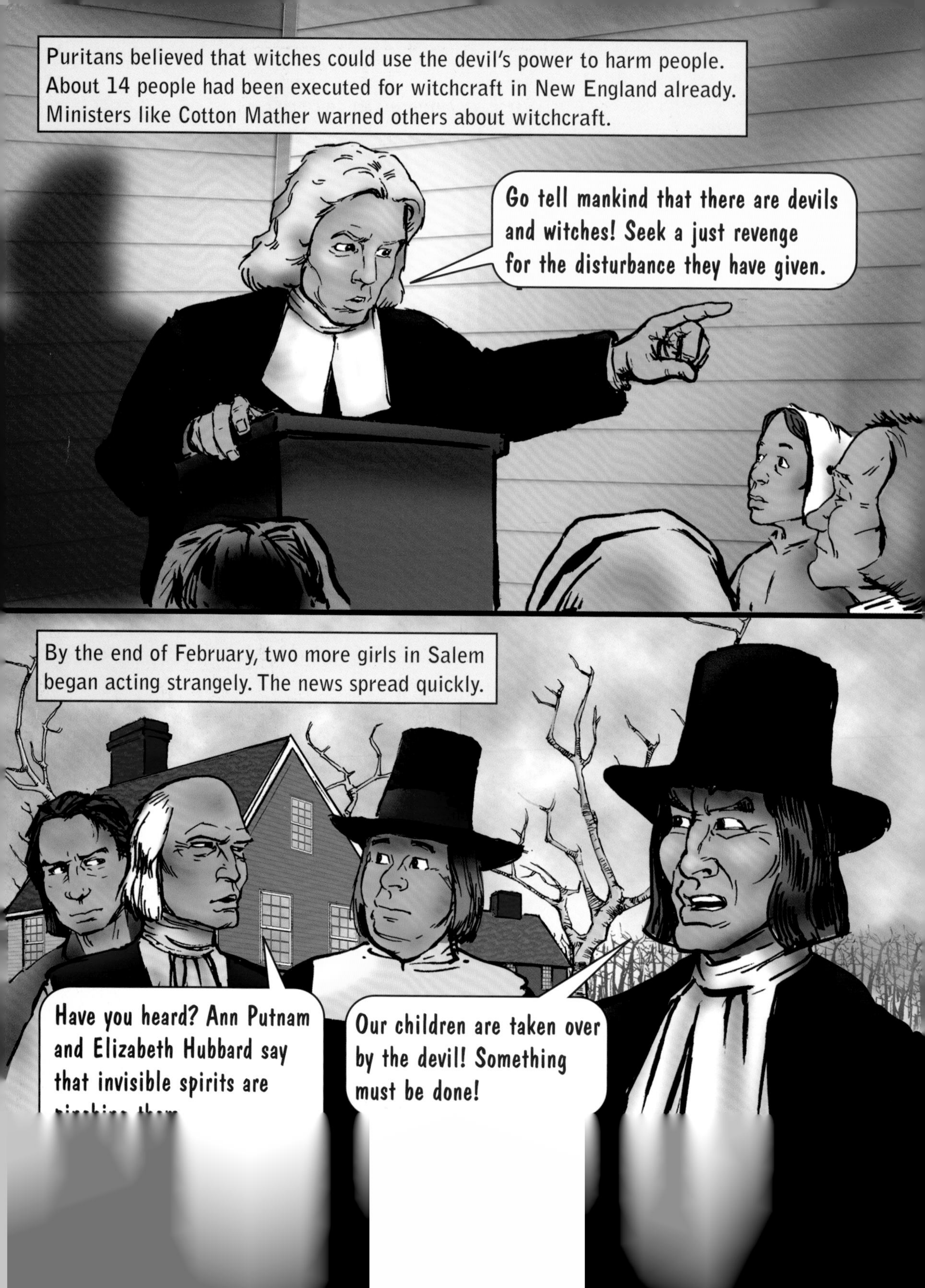
Puritans believed that witches could use the devil's power to harm people. About 14 people had been executed for witchcraft in New England already. Ministers like Cotton Mather warned others about witchcraft.
Go tell mankind that there are devils and witches! Seek a just revenge for the disturbance they have given.
By the end of February, two more girls in Salem began acting strangely. The news spread quickly.
Have you heard? Ann Putnam and Elizabeth Hubbard say that invisible spirits are
Our children are taken over by the devil! Something must be done!

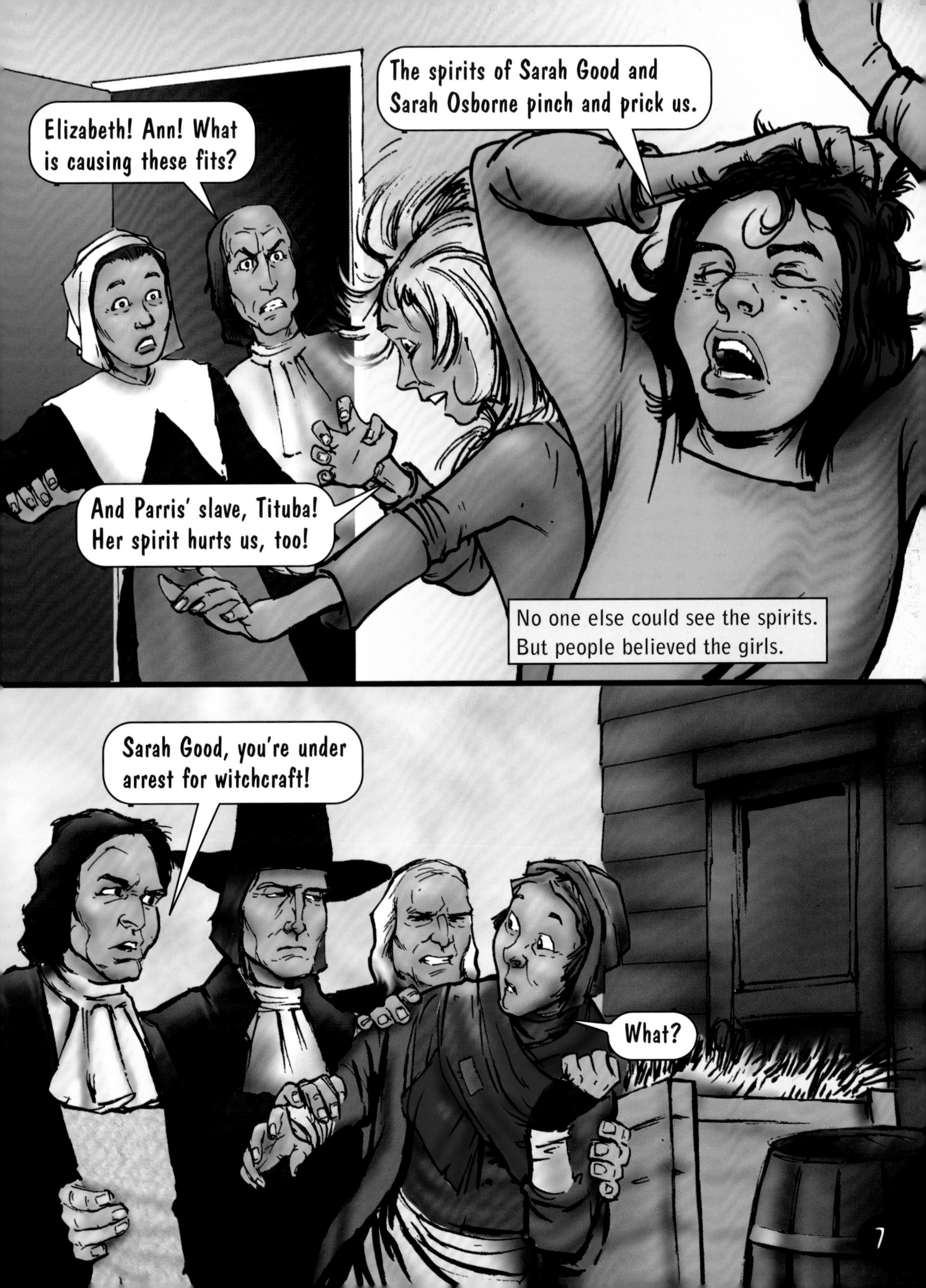
Elizabeth! Ann! What is causing these fits?
The spirits of Sarah Good and Sarah Osborne pinch and prick us.
And Parris' slave, Tituba! Her spirit hurts us, too!
No one else could see the spirits. But people believed the girls.
Sarah Good, you're under arrest for witchcraft!
What?

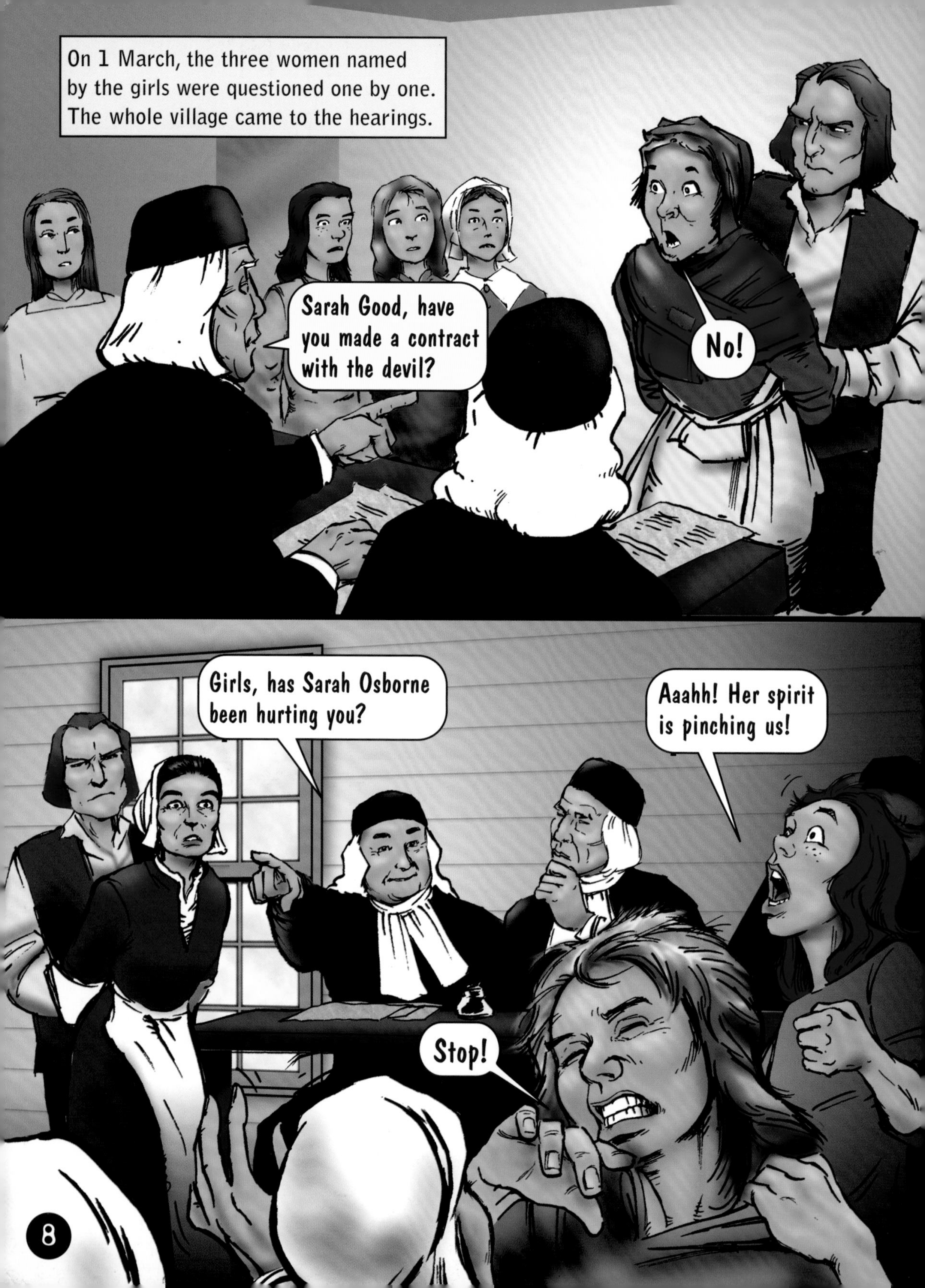

On 1 March, the three women named by the girls were questioned one by one. The whole village came to the hearings.
Sarah Good, have you made a contract with the devil?
No!
Girls, has Sarah Osborne been hurting you?
Aaahh! Her spirit is pinching us!
Stop!

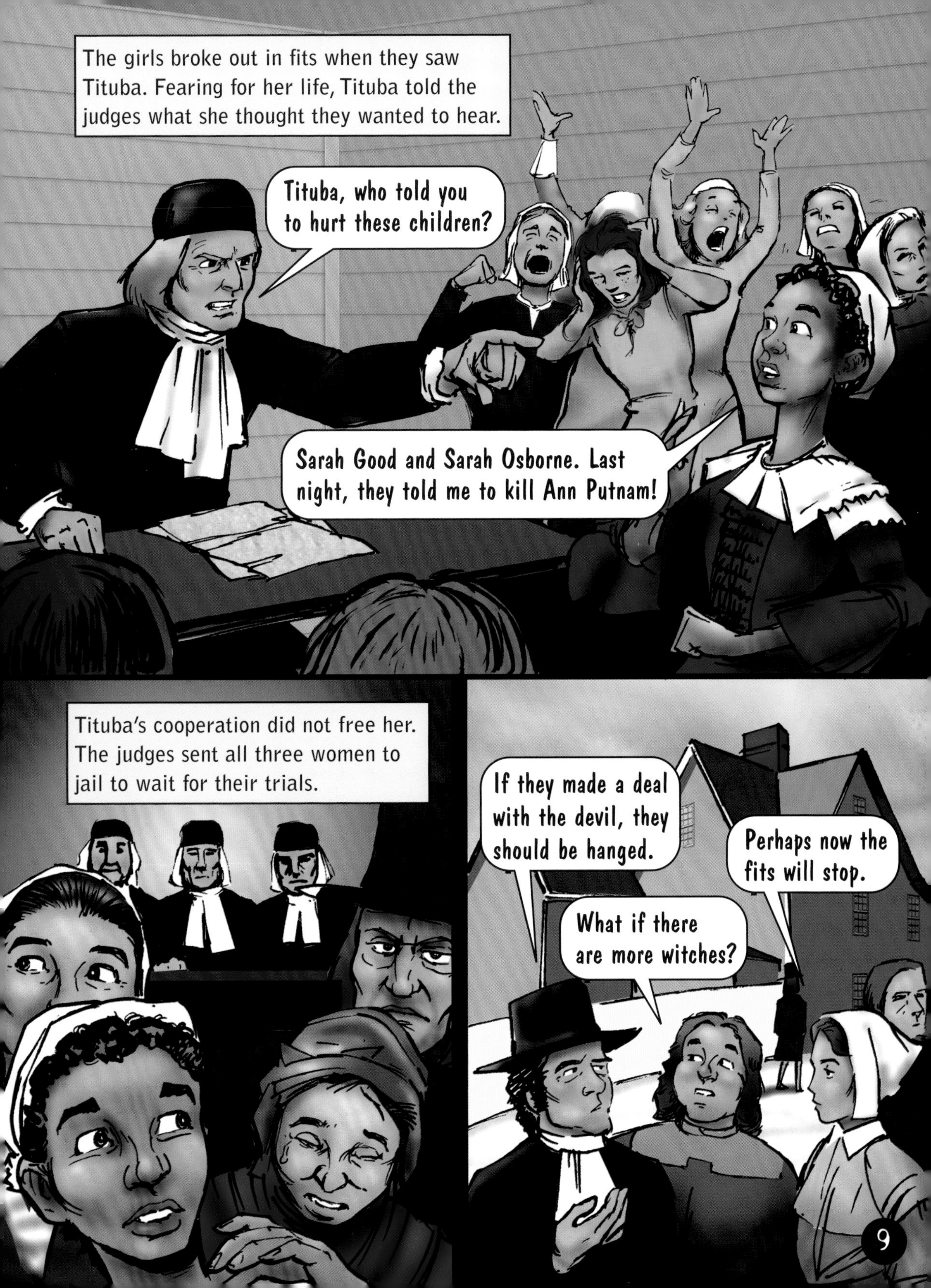
The girls broke out in fits when they saw Tituba. Fearing for her life, Tituba told the judges what she thought they wanted to hear.
Tituba, who told you to hurt these children?
Sarah Good and Sarah Osborne. Last night, they told me to kill Ann Putnam!
Tituba's cooperation did not free her. The judges sent all three women to jail to wait for their trials.
If they made a deal with the devil, they should be hanged.
Perhaps now the fits will stop.
What if there are more witches?

CHAPTER · 2

More Accusations

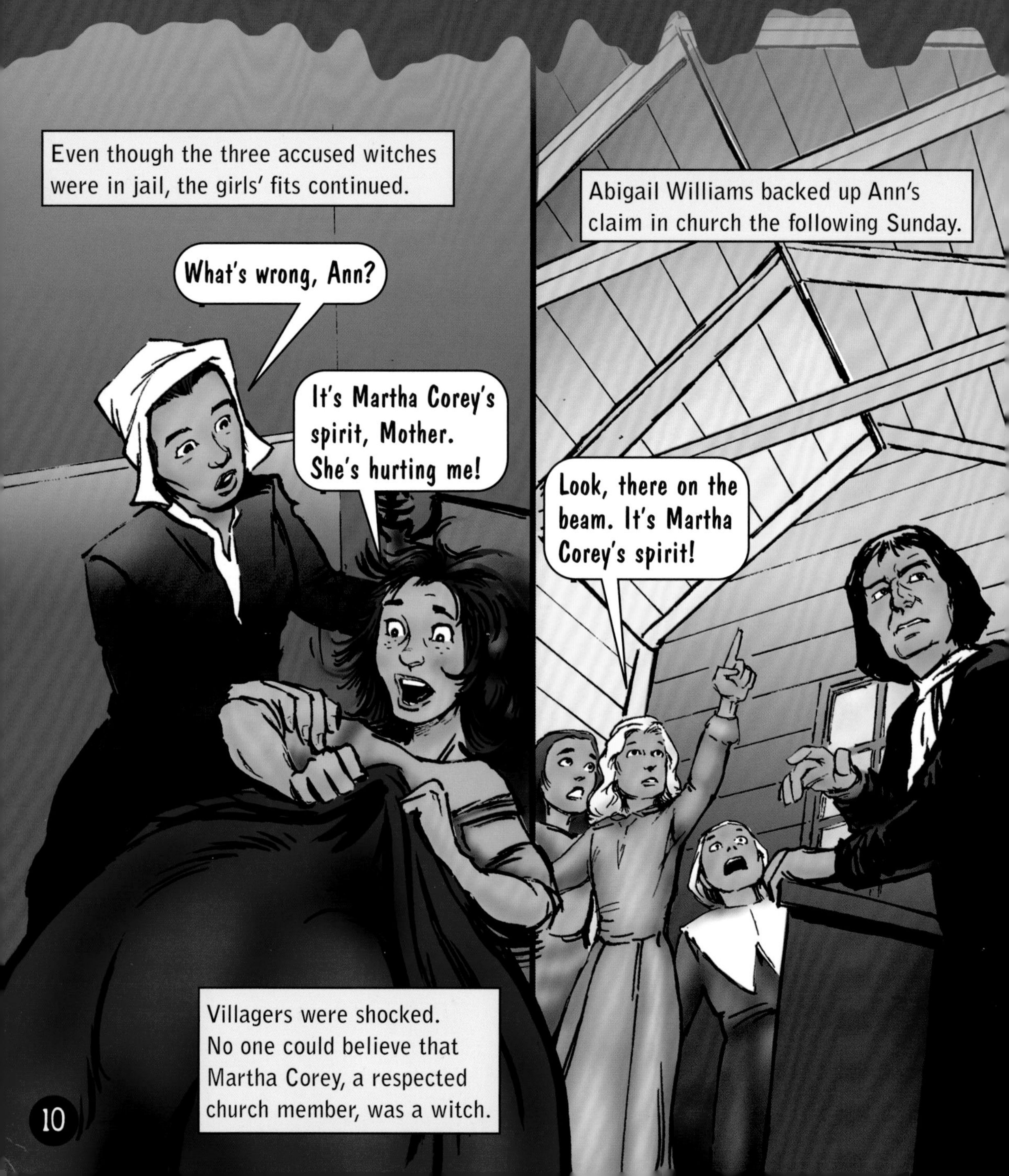
Even though the three accused witches were in jail, the girls' fits continued.
What's wrong, Ann?
It's Martha Corey's spirit, Mother. She's hurting me!
Villagers were shocked. No one could believe that Martha Corey, a respected church member, was a witch.
Abigail Williams backed up Ann's claim in church the following Sunday.
Look, there on the beam. It's Martha Corey's spirit!

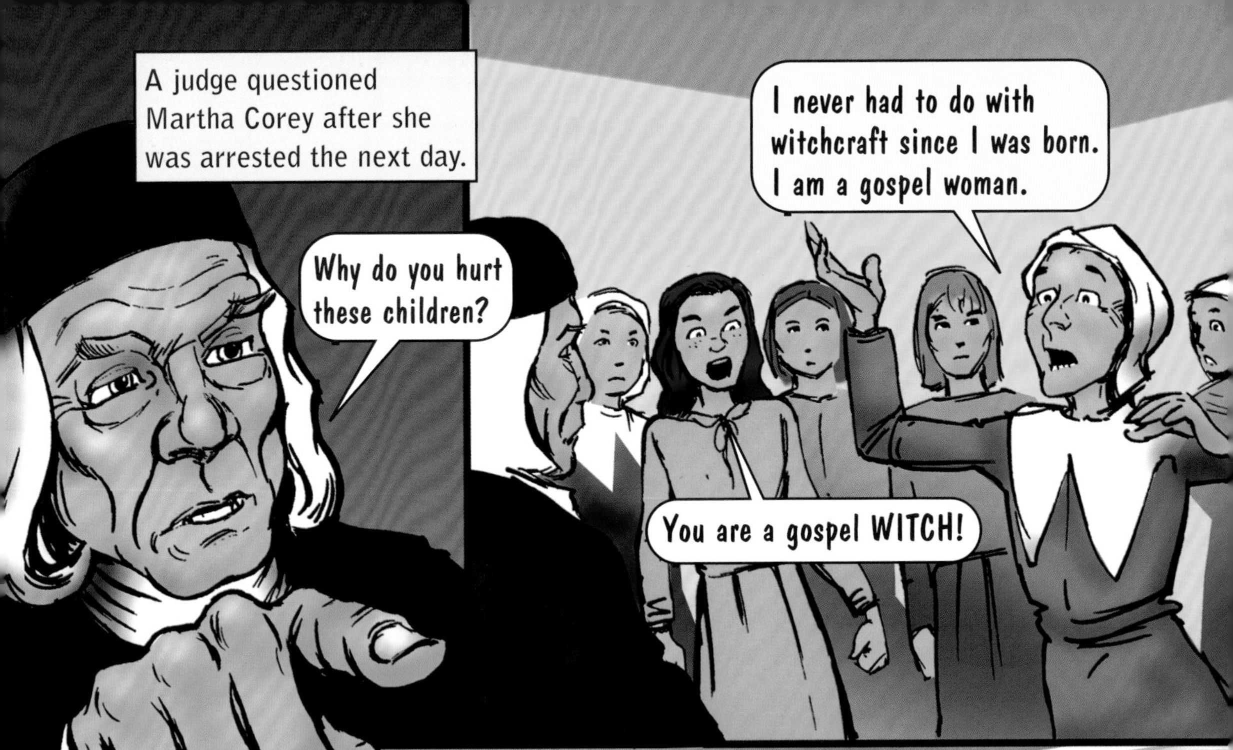
A judge questioned Martha Corey after she was arrested the next day.
Why do you hurt these children?
I never had to do with witchcraft since I was born. I am a gospel woman.
You are a gospel WITCH!

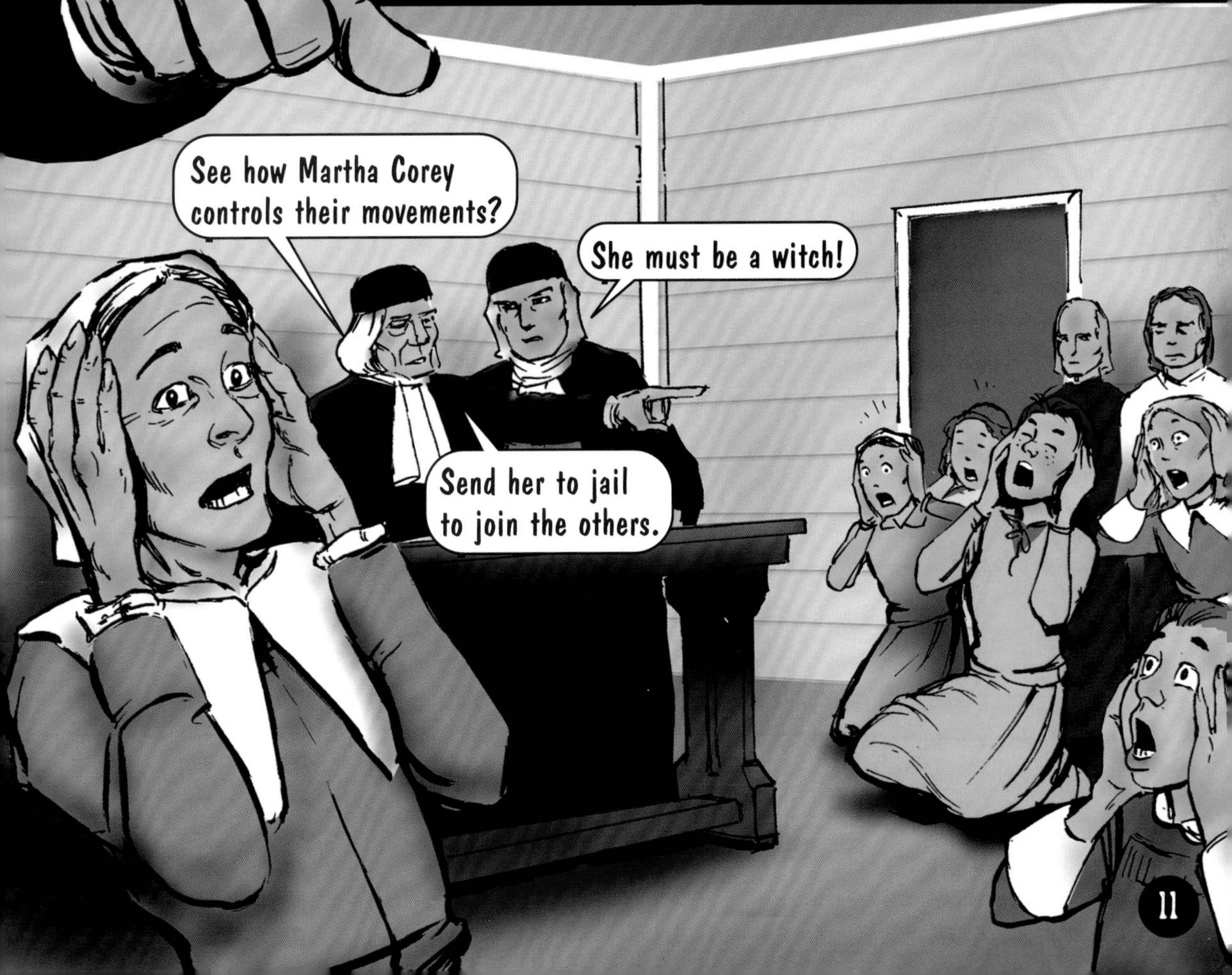
See how Martha Corey controls their movements?
She must be a witch!
Send her to jail to join the others.

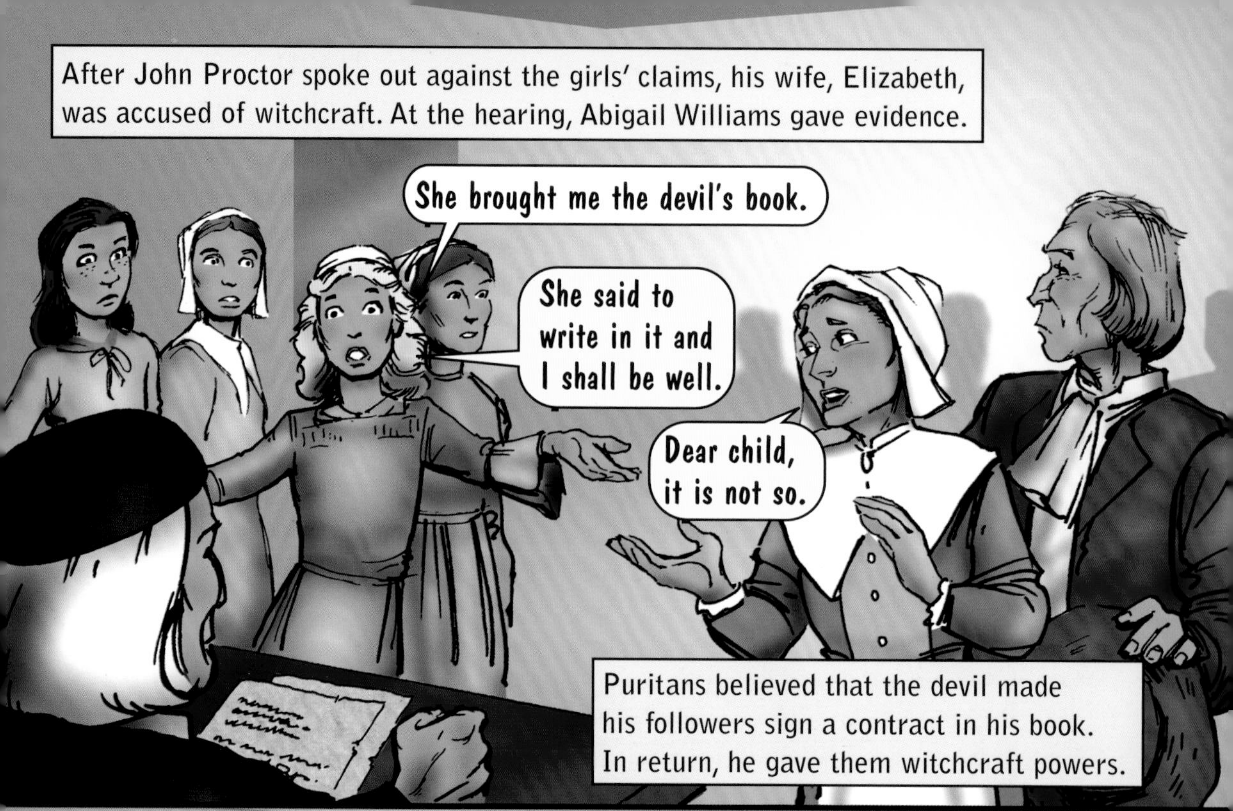
After John Proctor spoke out against the girls' claims, his wife, Elizabeth, was accused of witchcraft. At the hearing, Abigail Williams gave evidence.
She brought me the devil's book.
She said to write in it and I shall be well.
Dear child, it is not so.
Puritans believed that the devil made his followers sign a contract in his book. In return, he gave them witchcraft powers.

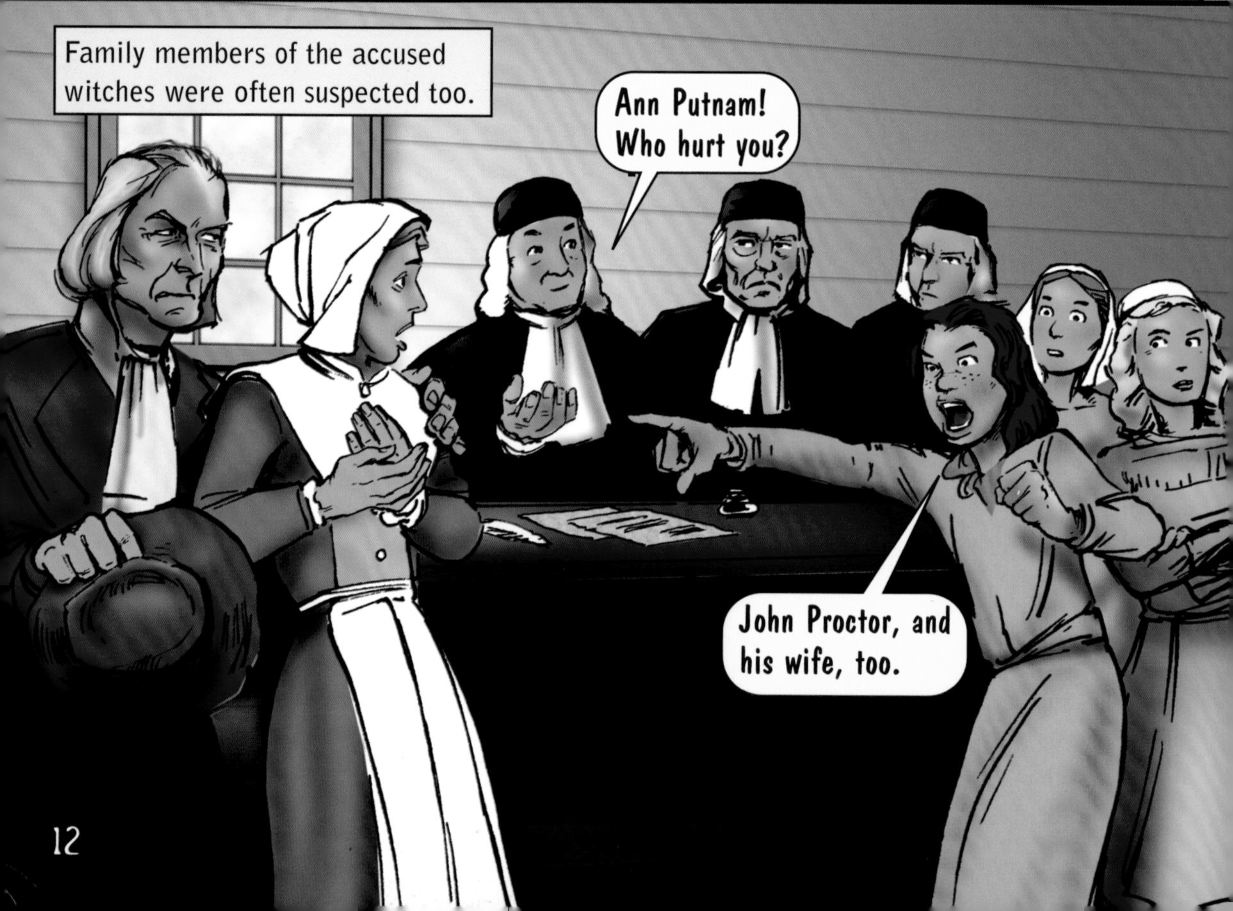
Family members of the accused witches were often suspected too.
Ann Putnam! Who hurt you?
John Proctor, and his wife, too.

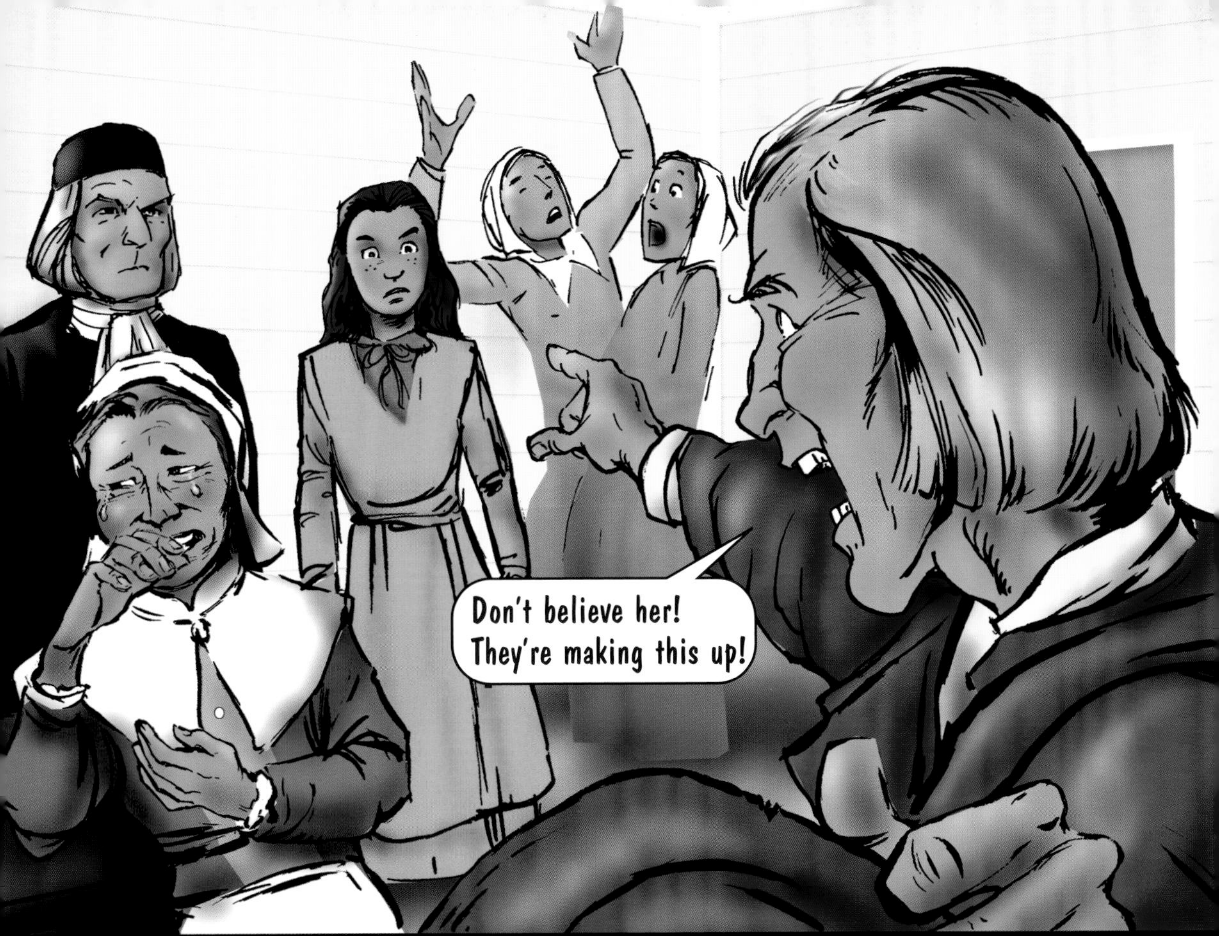
Don't believe her!
They're making this up!

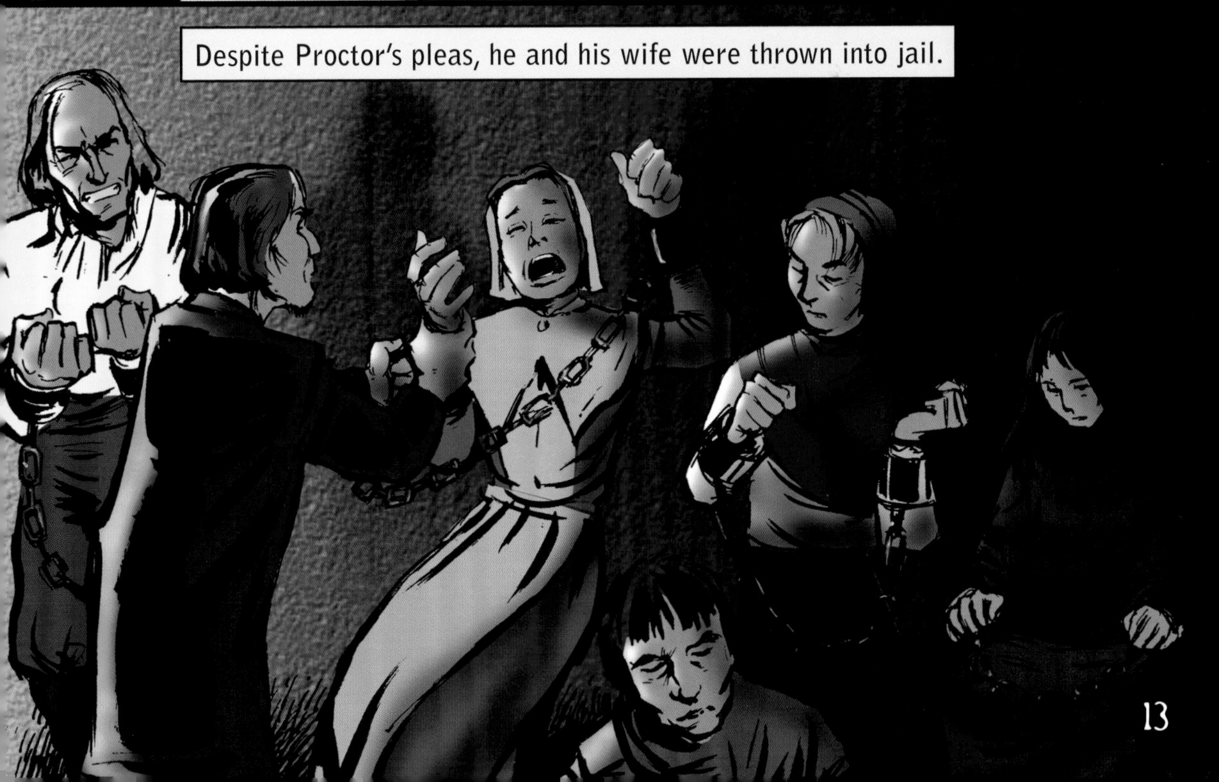
Despite Proctor's pleas, he and his wife were thrown into jail.

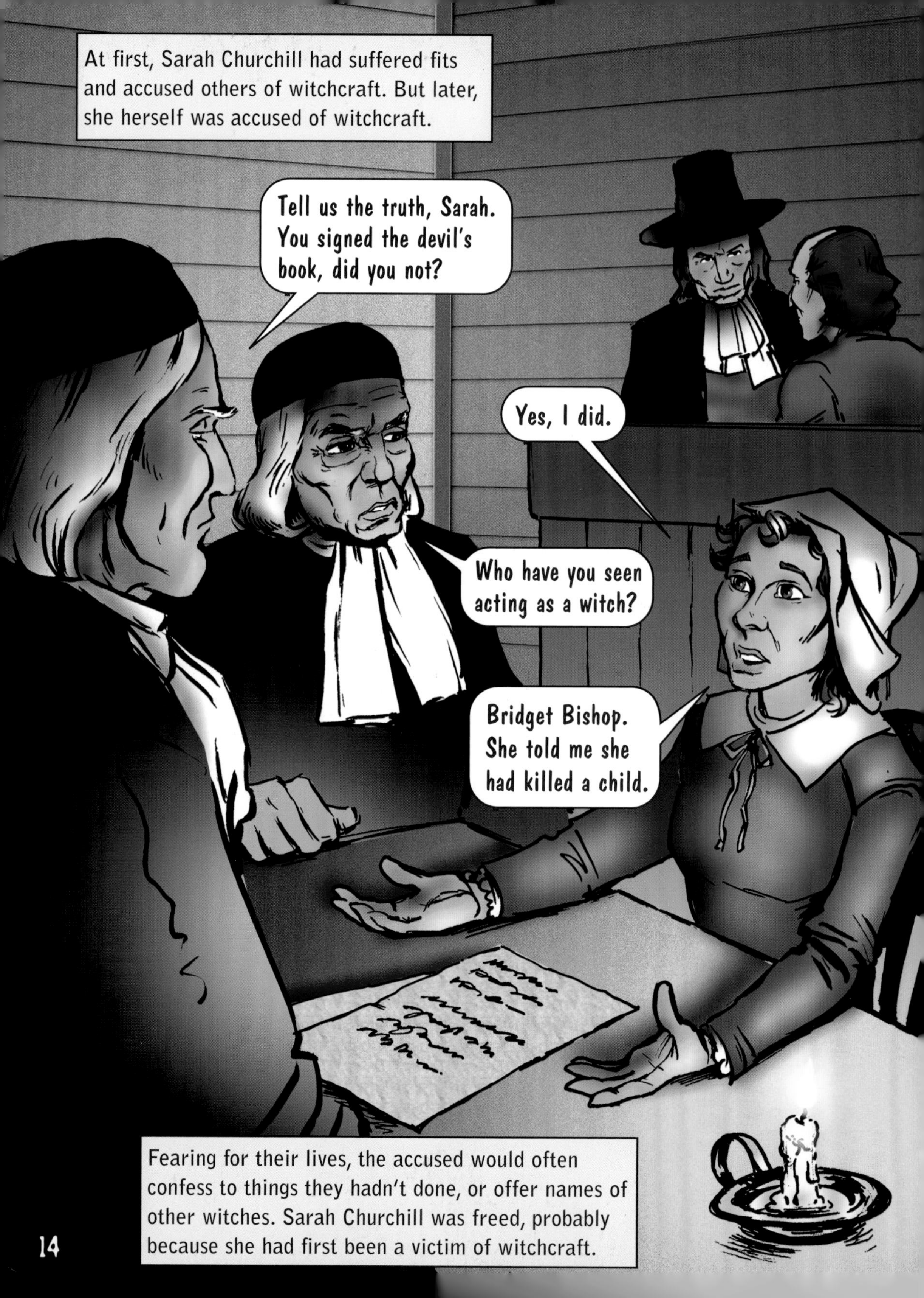
At first, Sarah Churchill had suffered fits and accused others of witchcraft. But later, she herself was accused of witchcraft.
Tell us the truth, Sarah. You signed the devil's book, did you not?
Yes, I did.
Who have you seen acting as a witch?
Bridget Bishop. She told me she had killed a child.
Fearing for their lives, the accused would often confess to things they hadn't done, or offer names of other witches. Sarah Churchill was freed, probably because she had first been a victim of witchcraft.

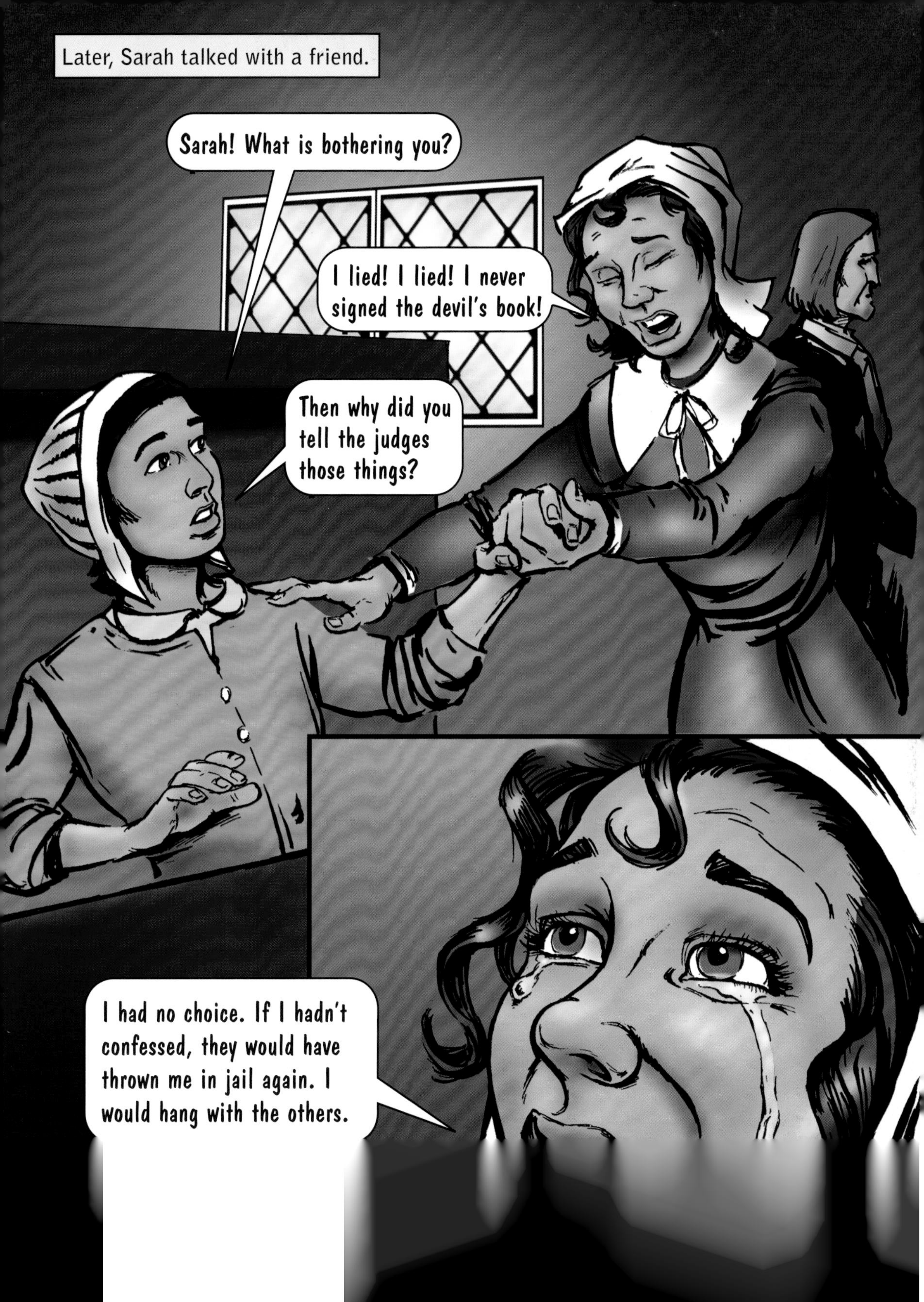
Later, Sarah talked with a friend.
Sarah! What is bothering you?
I lied! I lied! I never signed the devil's book!
Then why did you tell the judges those things?
I had no choice. If I hadn't confessed, they would have thrown me in jail again. I would hang with the others.

CHAPTER · 3

The Trials

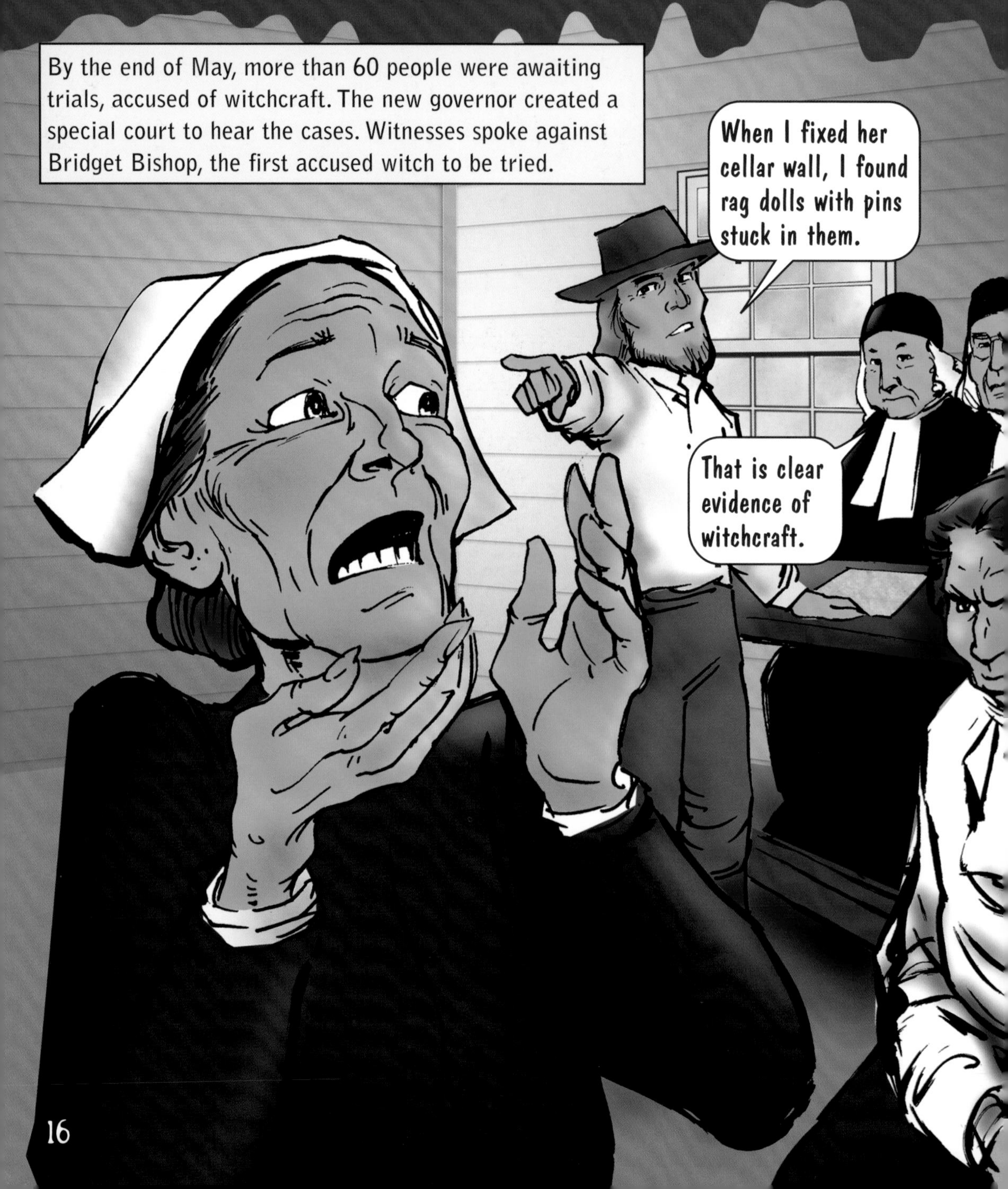
By the end of May, more than 60 people were awaiting trials, accused of witchcraft. The new governor created a special court to hear the cases. Witnesses spoke against Bridget Bishop, the first accused witch to be tried.
When I fixed her cellar wall, I found rag dolls with pins stuck in them.
That is clear evidence of witchcraft.

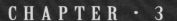

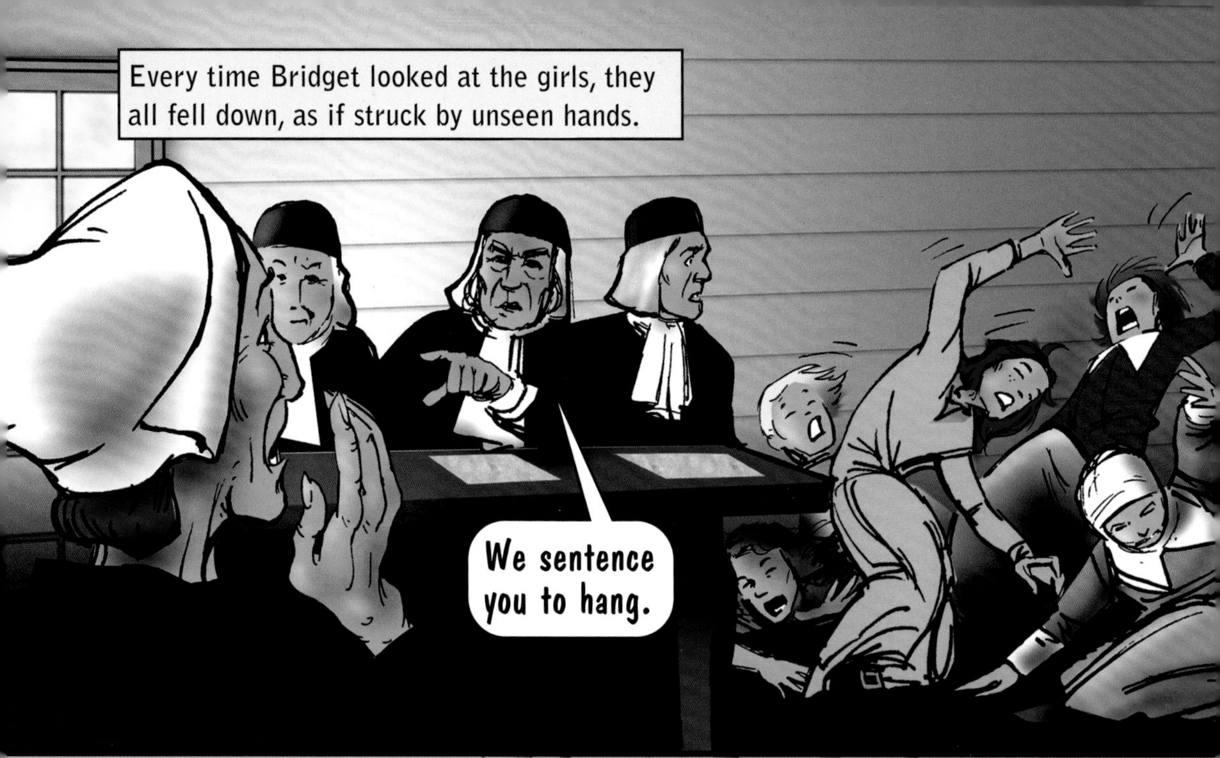
Every time Bridget looked at the girls, they all fell down, as if struck by unseen hands.
We sentence you to hang.

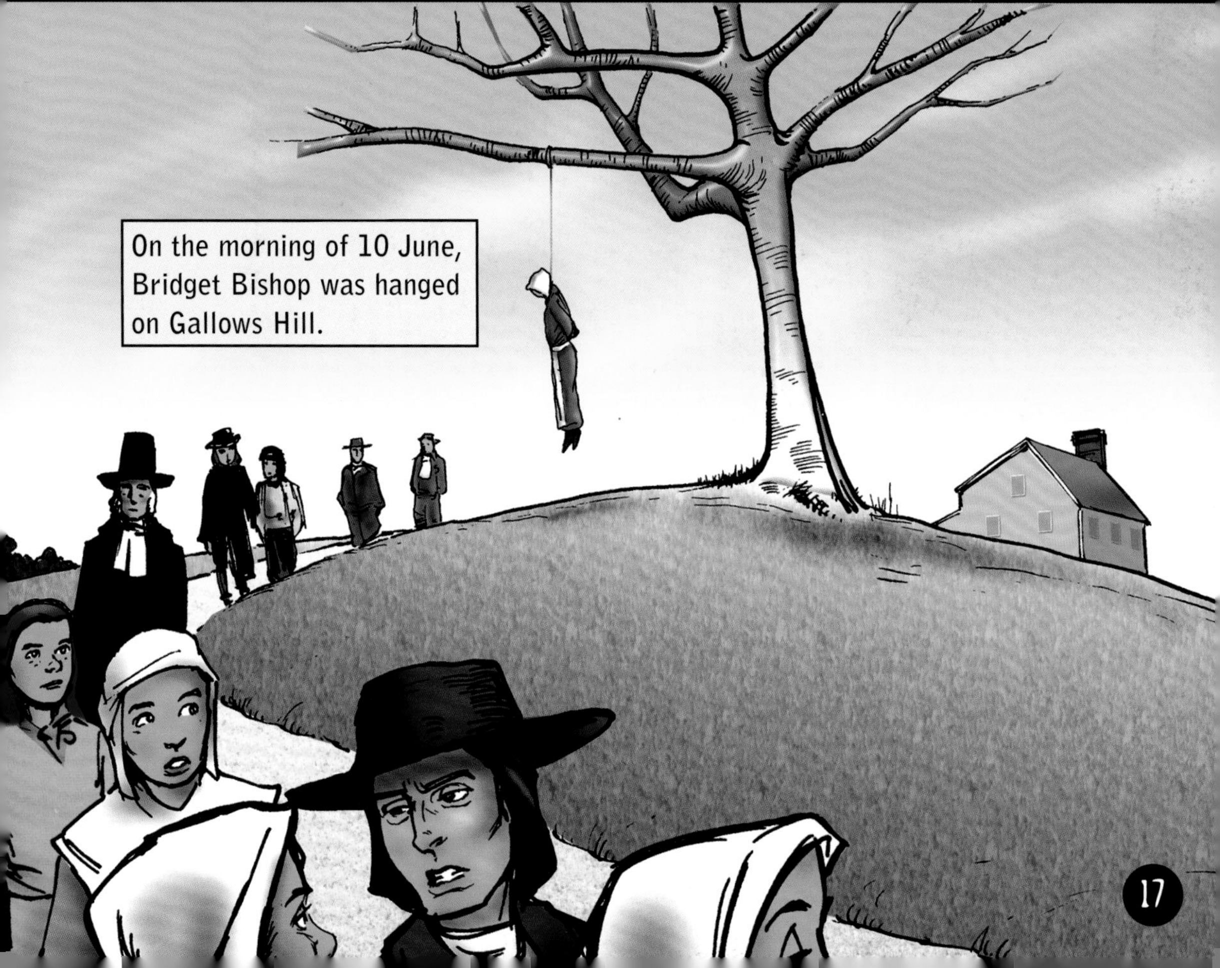
On the morning of 10 June, Bridget Bishop was hanged on Gallows Hill.

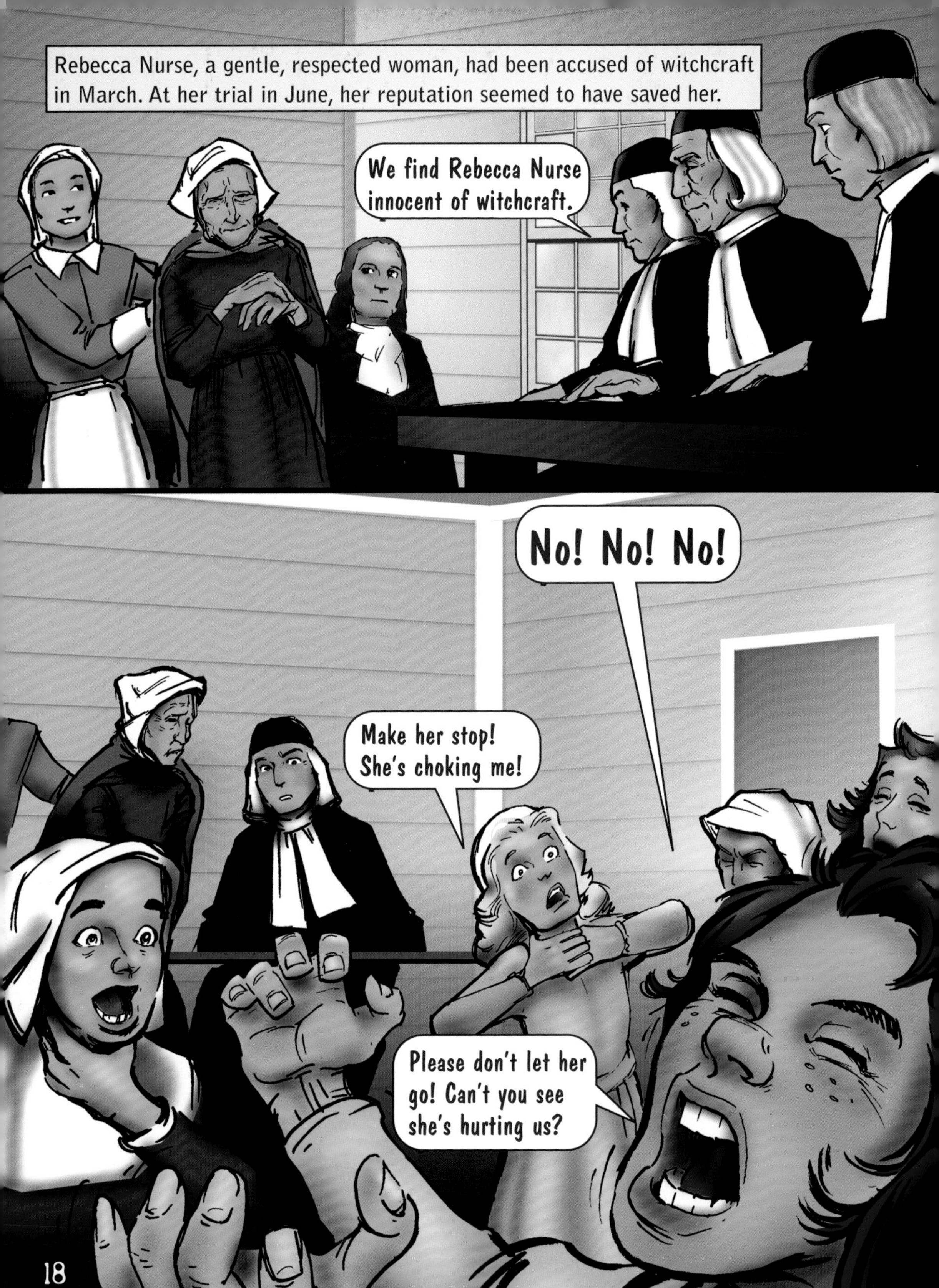
Rebecca Nurse, a gentle, respected woman, had been accused of witchcraft in March. At her trial in June, her reputation seemed to have saved her.
We find Rebecca Nurse innocent of witchcraft.
No! No! No!
Make her stop! She's choking me!
Please don't let her go! Can't you see she's hurting us?

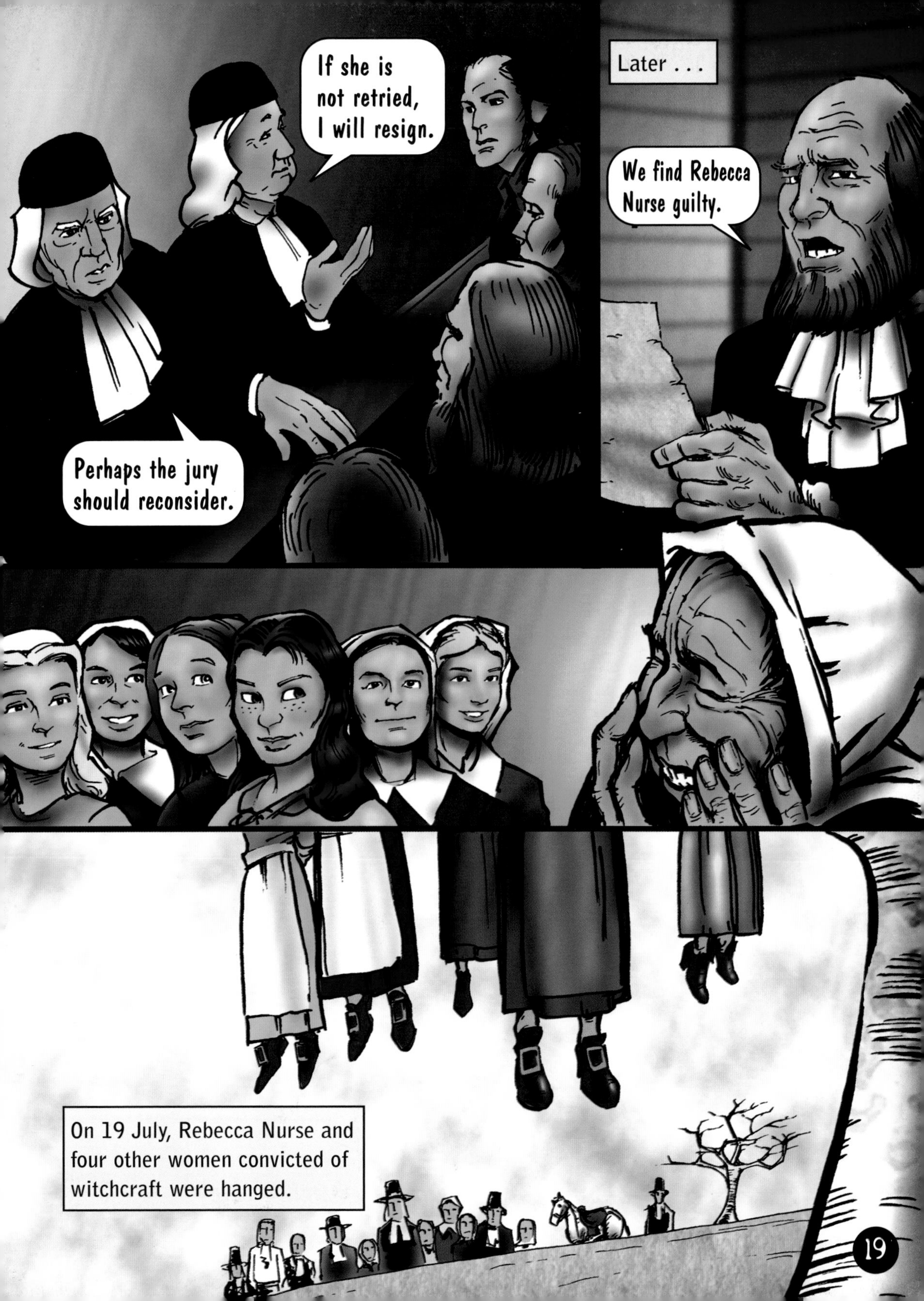
If she is not retried, I will resign.
Perhaps the jury should reconsider.
Later . . .
We find Rebecca Nurse guilty.
On 19 July, Rebecca Nurse and four other women convicted of witchcraft were hanged.

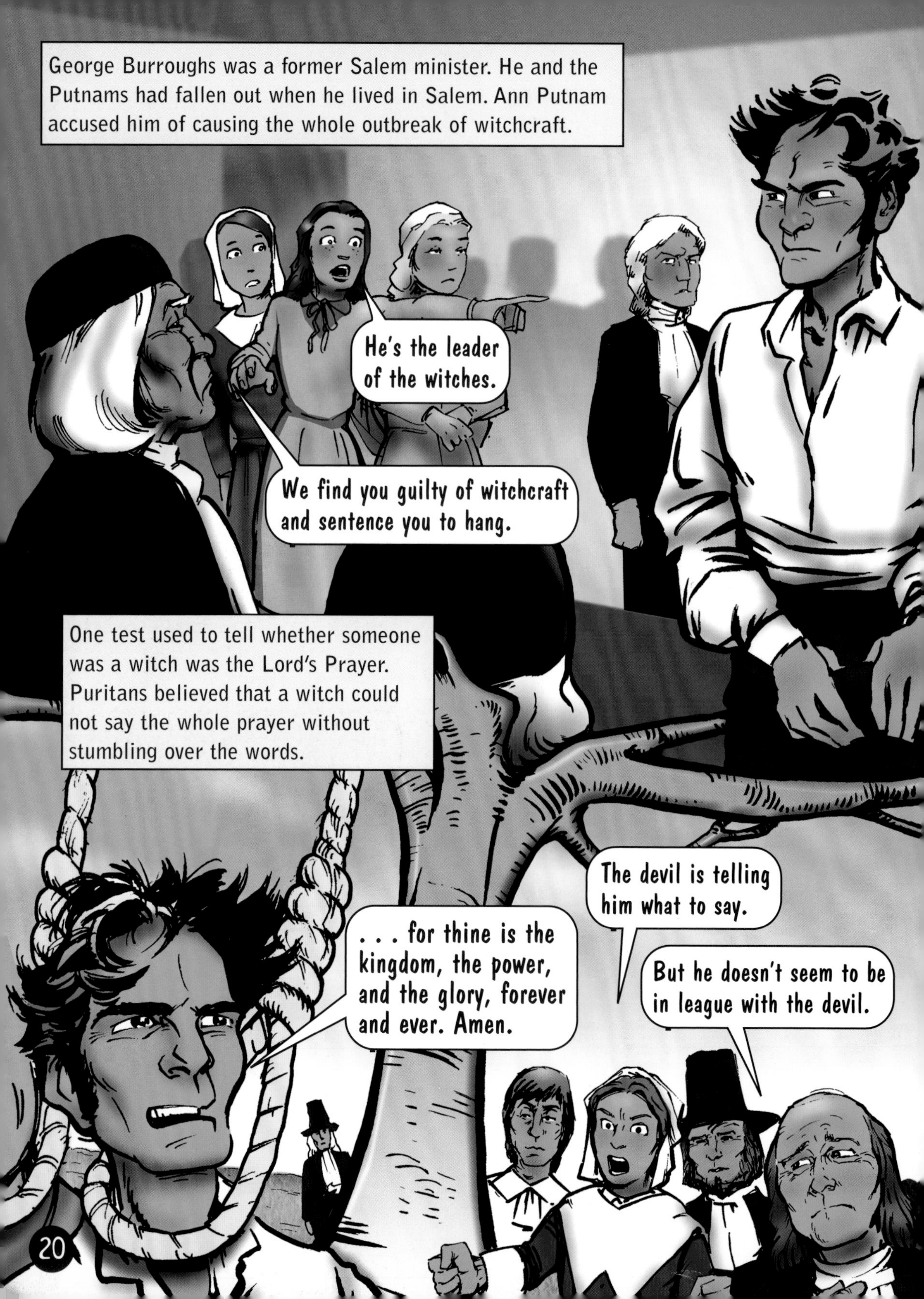
George Burroughs was a former Salem minister. He and the Putnams had fallen out when he lived in Salem. Ann Putnam accused him of causing the whole outbreak of witchcraft.
He's the leader of the witches.
We find you guilty of witchcraft and sentence you to hang.
One test used to tell whether someone was a witch was the Lord's Prayer. Puritans believed that a witch could not say the whole prayer without stumbling over the words.
. . . for thine is the kingdom, the power, and the glory, forever and ever. Amen.
The devil is telling him what to say.
But he doesn't seem to be in league with the devil.

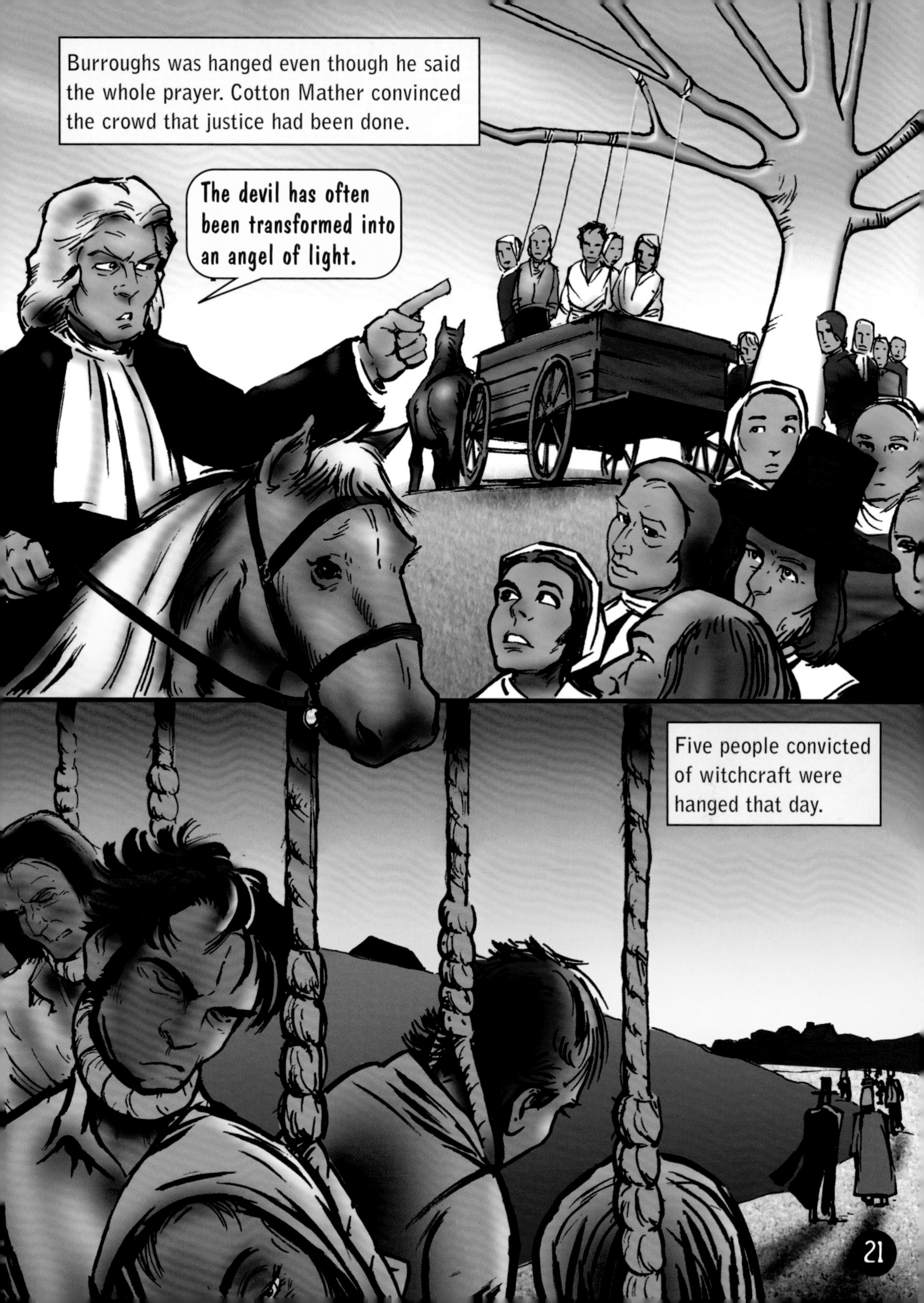
Burroughs was hanged even though he said the whole prayer. Cotton Mather convinced the crowd that justice had been done.
The devil has often been transformed into an angel of light.
Five people convicted of witchcraft were hanged that day.

CHAPTER · 4

Witchcraft Hysteria

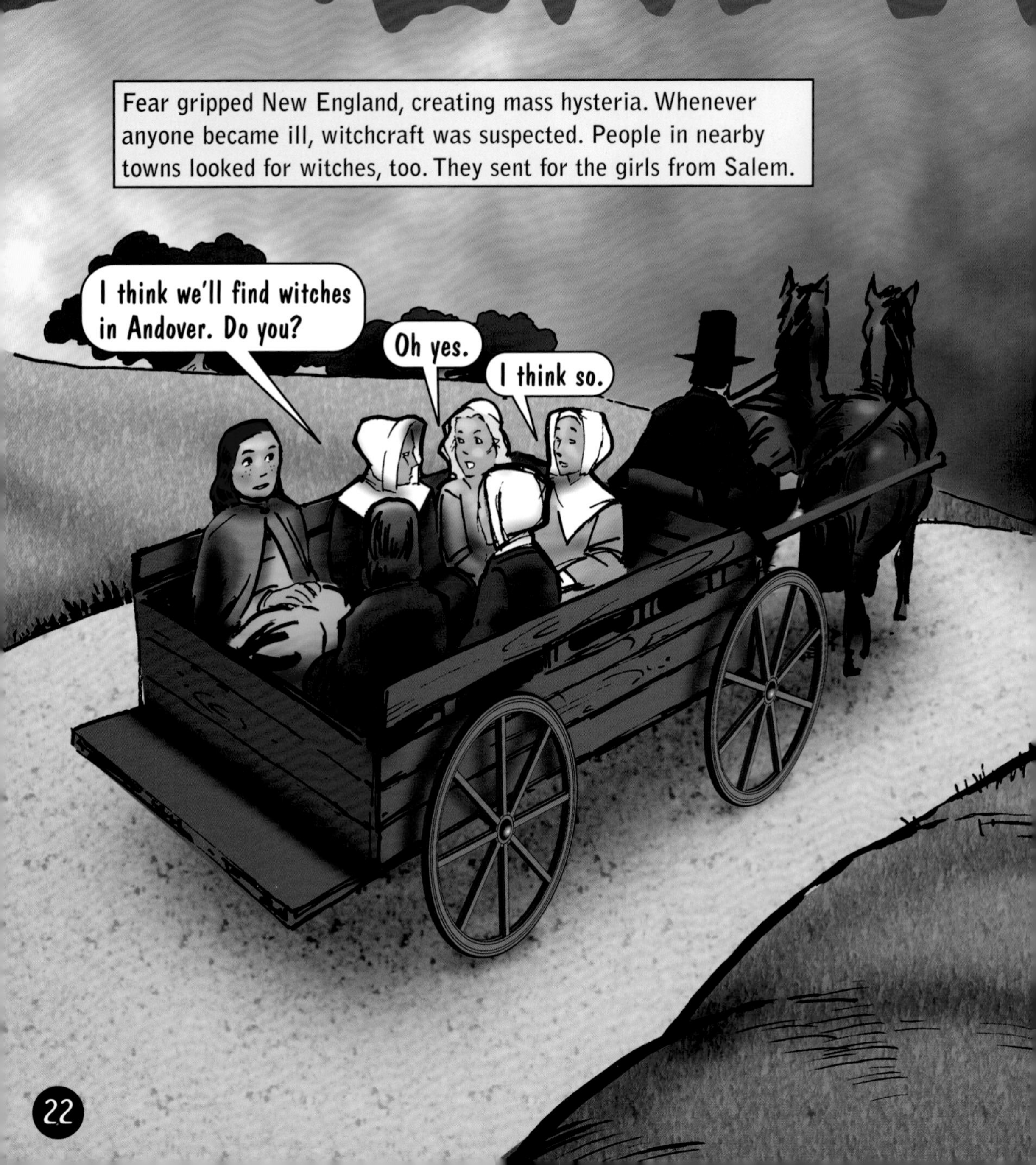
Fear gripped New England, creating mass hysteria. Whenever anyone became ill, witchcraft was suspected. People in nearby towns looked for witches, too. They sent for the girls from Salem.
I think we'll find witches in Andover. Do you?
Oh yes.
I think so.

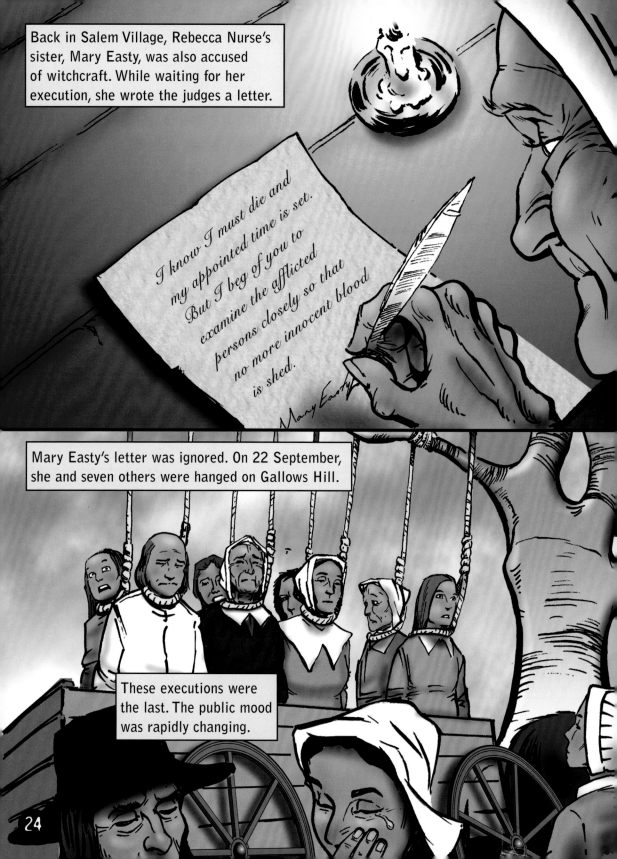

Back in Salem Village, Rebecca Nurse's sister, Mary Easty, was also accused of witchcraft. While waiting for her execution, she wrote the judges a letter.

I know I must die and my appointed time is set. But I beg of you to examine the afflicted persons closely so that no more innocent blood is shed.

Mary Easty

Mary Easty's letter was ignored. On 22 September, she and seven others were hanged on Gallows Hill.

These executions were the last. The public mood was rapidly changing.

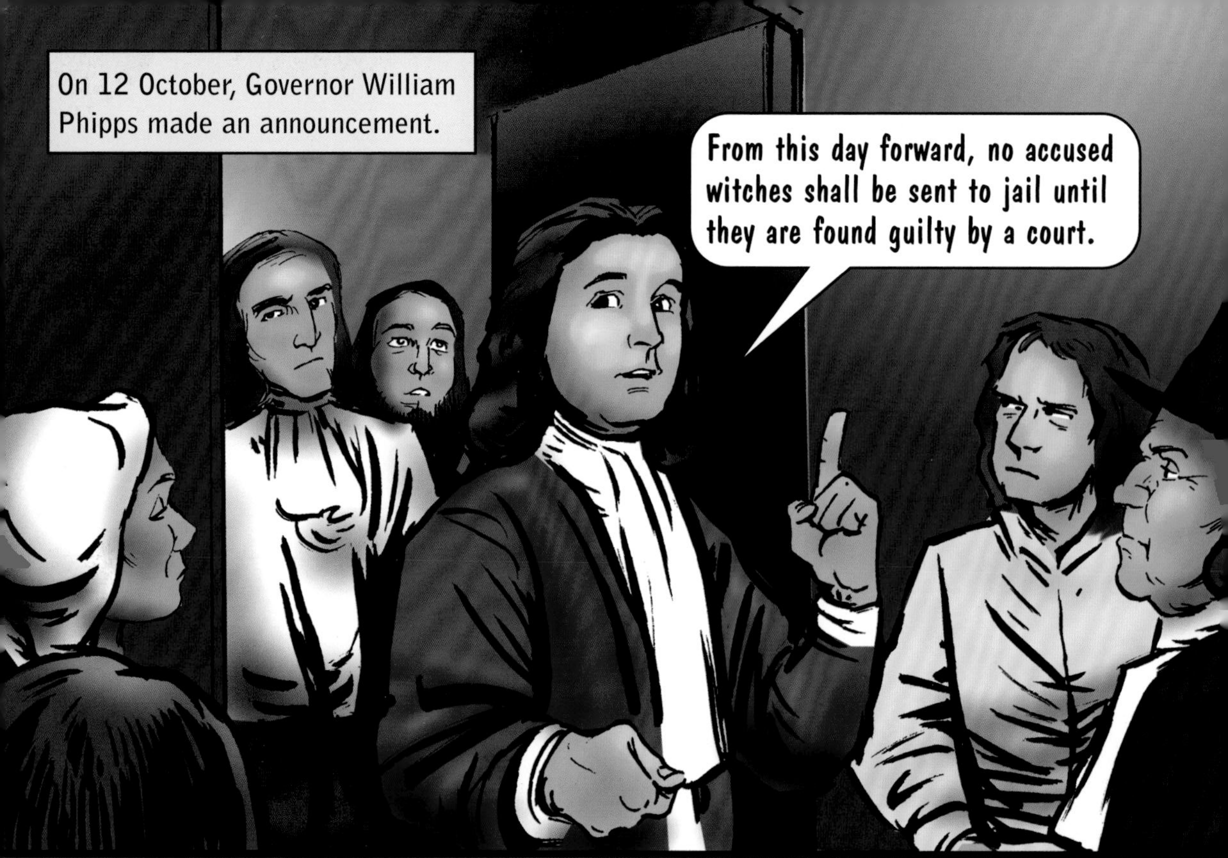
On 12 October, Governor William Phipps made an announcement.
From this day forward, no accused witches shall be sent to jail until they are found guilty by a court.

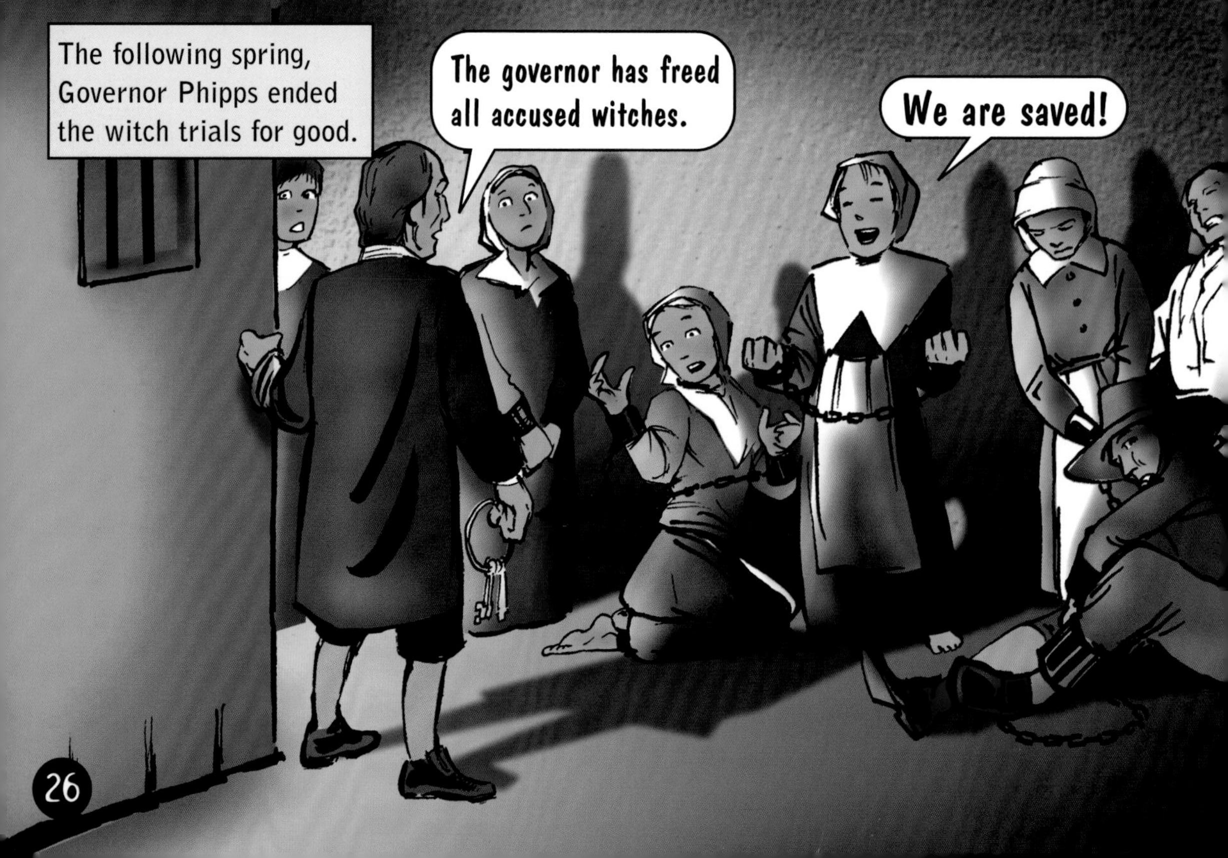
The following spring, Governor Phipps ended the witch trials for good.
The governor has freed all accused witches.
We are saved!

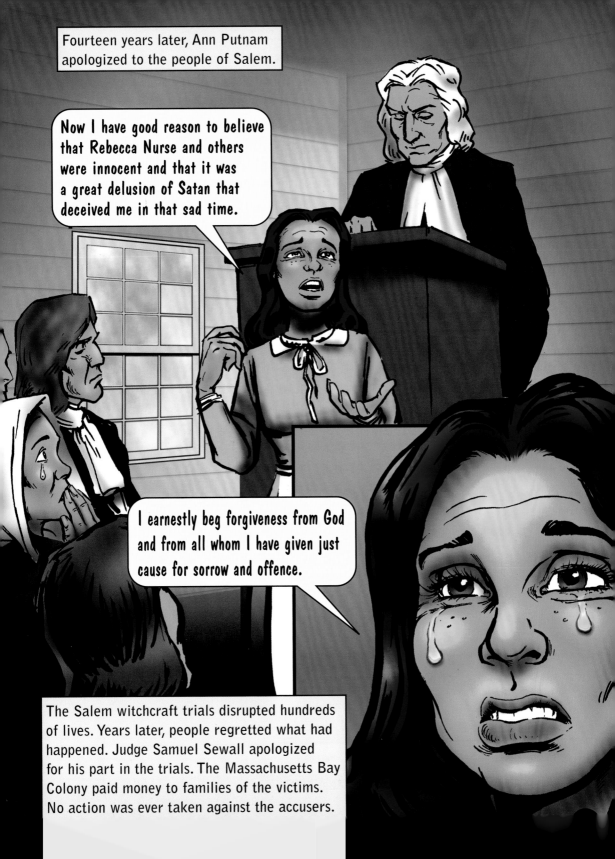

The Salem Witch Trials

✳ ## Salem witch trials statistics

Number of accusers:	19
Number of people arrested as witches:	about 150
Number of arrested people convicted:	28
Number of convicted people hanged:	19
Other deaths:	4 died in jail
	1 man crushed to death

✳ ## Dates of hangings

10 June 1692	Bridget Bishop
19 July 1692	Sarah Good, Elizabeth Howe, Susannah Martin, Rebecca Nurse, and Sarah Wilds
19 August 1692	Reverend George Burroughs, Martha Carrier, George Jacobs, John Proctor, and John Willard
22 September 1692	Martha Corey, Mary Easty, Alice Parker, Mary Parker, Ann Pudeator, Wilmot Redd, Margaret Scott, and Samuel Wardwell

The Theories

For more than 300 years, historians have tried to explain what caused the witchcraft outbreak in Salem in 1692.

✳ Writing shortly after the trials, Robert Calef thought the accusers were faking their acts. He blamed ministers like Cotton Mather for creating a climate of mass hysteria.

✳ Paul Boyer and Stephen Nissenbaum believe that power struggles and family feuds made people accuse others of witchcraft.

✳ Laurie Winn Carlson believed that a disease called encephalitis caused the girls' fits. The disease, spread by mosquitoes, can cause fever, confusion, and seizures.

✳ Chadwick Hansen thought that some people in Salem really did practise witchcraft, and people were very afraid of it.

✳ Bernard Rosenthal argued that the stories of witchcraft were made up. His reasons included jealousy, getting rid of personal enemies, and people truly believing in witches.

✳ A recent historian, Mary Beth Norton, blamed the climate of fear on wars with Native Americans. When the wars began going badly, fearful New Englanders searching for a reason blamed witchcraft.

Glossary

afflicted affected by a disease or condition, such as witchcraft

execution act of putting someone to death as punishment for a crime

hearing meeting held by judges to see if there is enough evidence to hold a trial

Lord's Prayer prayer said by Christians. This prayer appears in the Bible.

mass hysteria overwhelming fear or panic felt by many people at one time

Puritans group of Protestants in England during the 1500s and 1600s who wanted simple church services and enforced a strict moral code. Many Puritans fled England and settled in North America.

Internet Sites

school.discoveryeducation.com/schooladventures/
salemwitchtrials/
On this website, you can read about the story of the witch hunt and some of the key people involved.

www.pbs.org/wnet/secrets/previous_seasons/case_salem/
index.html
On this website, you'll find an interactive map of Salem Village, with information on all the main characters and a timeline of events. Click on the "View questions for students" link to test yourself on what you've learned.

Find Out More

Salem Witch Trials: Colonial Life (American History Through Primary Sources), Sean Price (Raintree, 2008)

The Salem Witch Trials (We the People), Michael Burgan (Compass Point Books, 2005)

You Wouldn't Want to Be a Salem Witch!: Bizarre Accusations You'd Rather Not Face, Jim Pipe and David Salariya (Franklin Watts, 2009)

Bibliography

A Delusion of Satan: The Full Story of the Salem Witch Trials, Frances Hill (Doubleday, 1995)

The Devil in Massachusetts: A Modern Inquiry into the Salem Witch Trials, Marion Lena Starkey (Alfred A. Knopf, 1949). Reprinted with introduction by Aldous Huxley (Time Life Books, 1982).

In the Devil's Snare: The Salem Witchcraft Crisis of 1692, Mary Beth Norton (Alfred A. Knopf, 2002)

Memorable Providences Relating to Witchcraft and Possession, Cotton Mather (Edinburgh, 1697)

The Salem Witchcraft Papers: Verbatim Transcripts of the Legal Documents of the Salem Witchcraft Outbreak of 1692, Paul Boyer and Stephen Nissenbaum (University of Vriginia Library, 2003) http://etext.virginia.edu/salem/witchcraft/texts/transcripts.html.

Index